Ken Wachsberger's

Puns and Word Plays
for the Job Seeker

Illustrations by
Thomas Petiet

Azenphony Press
Ann Arbor, MI

Published by
Azenphony Press
PO Box 130884
Ann Arbor, MI 48113-0884
U.S.A.
info@azenphonypress.com
www.azenphonypress.com
(734) 635-0577

Ken Wachsberger's Puns and Word Plays for the Job Seeker, 1st edition
© April 15, 2018, the day Dad would have been 100, by Ken Wachsberger

ISBN 978-0-945531-11-1 (pbk)
ISBN 978-0-945531-12-8 (ebook)

Cover, graphics, and typesetting by Thomas Petiet, Concept Studio

All rights reserved. Without limiting the rights under copyright reserved above, no part of this publication may be reproduced, stored in or introduced into a retrieval system, or transmitted, in any form, or by any means (electronic, mechanical, photocopying, recording, or otherwise) without the prior written permission of both the copyright owner and the above publisher of this book.

This book is dedicated to Dad
for not holding back
even the bad puns

And Mom for suppressing her groans
and loving us all

Introduction

A pun came to me one night as I was fading into sleep: "You'll never get rich being a member of the loyal opposition, but you'll earn a dissent living." I thought it was hilarious so I posted it on Facebook the next day to see if I would get a reaction. Lots of funny responses told me I had an audience.

So I posted a variation, which came to me the next night: "You'll never get rich living on a mountaintop and working in the valley, but you'll earn a descent living." I got more favorable responses. (In the pun world, a groan counts as a favorable response.)

For about two weeks, I posted puns about job seeking and had puns thrown back at me by my Facebook friends. Somewhere along the way, I realized I had to stop so I didn't get typecast, but I continued accumulating puns on my own.

The result is *Ken Wachsberger's Puns and Word Plays for the Job Seeker*.

I couldn't help it; they came to me. It was inevitable.

As a child, sitting around the kitchen table with any combination of Dad, my three brothers, and Mom, no meal ever ended without our having survived at least one battle of puns set off most often by one person's accidental pun (those were generally the best) and the resulting burst of puns from all corners of the table.

Dad loved them. My brothers and I all loved them. Mom grimaced through them all but I think she loved them, too, because they came from her family as we dined and laughed together.

My deepest gratitude to cartoonist and graphic artist Tom Petiet for masterfully introducing visuals and design to what would otherwise have been a long list.

Tom is legendary in the Ann Arbor area not only as a graphic artist and cartoonist but as the founder, with his wife Pat, of the Comic Opera Guild, a grassroots gang of zany actors and actresses who have performed little-known, long-forgotten comic operas for over forty years, often with scripts translated into English from French by Tom himself.

It is my honor to have Tom translate my words to cartoon.

Who says the economy is getting better?
Not my friends, who have tried
everything they could to land
a decent-paying gig.

Some made it; others didn't.

Here are their touching testimonials,
their horror stories and close calls,
their hard-luck adventures,
and their words of wisdom
for job seekers everywhere.

You'll never get rich being a member of the loyal opposition, but you'll earn a dissent living.

You'll never get rich living
on a mountaintop and
working in the valley,
but you'll earn a
descent living.

You'll never get rich being a
tour guide in a museum,
but you'll earn a
docent living.

I almost got stuck working
as a haberdasher, but
I got out just in time.

It was sew clothes.

I was fired for stealing from the art gallery's cash register, but I was framed.

My plan to drive
a tow truck
went off
without
a hitch.

I was offered a position in a men's choir but I didn't feel comfortable with the tenor of the group.

Aida thought it wouldn't be hard to find a job as an opera singer, but I really made a mezzo my auditions (tenor eleven of them).

I didn't think I was qualified
to be an editor, but my
teacher convinced me
with the old
caret and stick
approach.

I really had no desire to inherit
my dad's jewelry store,
but he used the old
karat and stick
approach.

When I told the boss
at the orchard that
I was afraid to
climb trees,
he told me to
get a pear.

I got a job in a men's wear business because of family ties.

That suited me fine.

I tried working at a French restaurant, but it bored the crepe out of me.

I competed with other
applicants to be
a hair stylist
but I didn't
make the cut.

The next day I tried again
at another salon
and got a
permanent
position.

I liked their style
and we
clearly gelled.

I got into fights while trying to secure our ship for the night so I was required to take a course in anchor management.

My plan to find investors
in a butcher shop
fell through because
it had no meat.

The head chef at the vegetarian restaurant was the evilest person I ever met.

It was like working for seitan.

I escaped with my life after apprenticing with a mystic poet.

Who knew he was ethereal killer?

I felt so bad about rejecting my uncle's offer to sell cars that I agreed instead to help rent them.

It was the leased I could do.

I was offered a job
as a ceramicist
but the offer
was a crock.

I applied for a job
as a contortionist
but they didn't have
a position for me.

I'm not sure I would make
a good trial lawyer.

The jury is still out
on that one.

I wasn't scared of my forestry boss' yelling because I thought it was all bark.

The next day he
gave me
the ax.

So I boughed out.

I believed the boss
when he promised
me a job designing
home exteriors
but it was
all a façade.

I tried to get a job at
the morgue but it was
a grave mistake.

I faced stiff competition.

The scenery while working in Paris was beautiful.

I got a real Eiffel.

My attempt to become
an S&M expert
was bound to fail,
even after they
whipped me
into shape.

I loved being a tree trimmer.

I could always count on
my boss going out
on a limb for me.

I worked at the watch factory
until my boss ticked me off
and I knew it was
time to leave.

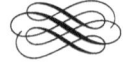

On my last day, my fellow
workers gave me
a big hand.

There's nothing like owning
a package-delivery outlet.

I was the master
of my freight.

I lasted a week at a German restaurant.

It was the wurst job I ever had.

The contractor hinted
at giving me a job on
his road crew but
he never gave me
a concrete offer.

When I was a lad
I wanted to be a
Merchant Marine
but that ship
sailed long ago.

I wasn't really qualified
to work as a
yoga instructor
but I applied
anyway.

It was a stretch.

I was never detail-oriented enough to be a good estate attorney.

I didn't like splitting heirs.

I knew I was about
to get fired from the
ice cream parlor
when my friend
gave me the
inside scoop.

I knew I was about to get fired
from the weight loss clinic
when I got the skinny
on the next week's
work schedule.

There's nothing humerus
about being an
orthopedic surgeon.

When I left the
police force,
they said I was
a copout.

I felt safe working with
the chiropractor.

Even when I made a mistake
I knew he had my back.

But then he let me go.
He said I wasn't well
adjusted but he was
too spineless to give
me the real reason.

I had a chance to be
both a policeman
and a fireman.

I chose the ladder.

I had a good offer to be
a forest ranger but
it wasn't rock solid
and it would have
meant uprooting
my family.

I couldn't cut it
as a surgeon.

I was passed over
for a role in our
local opera
because
I didn't
give a fach.

Should I pursue a career in kayaking or canoeing?

This is definitely an "either oar" scenario.

I couldn't decide if I wanted to
be an anesthesiologist
or a miner.

It was an ether/ore decision.

I loved being a cardiologist.

I'd do it again in a heartbeat.

Or something else
in that vein.

The head of the department
where I taught was nuts.

She didn't have all
of her faculties.

My job as an antique
auto salesman
fit me to a T.

I hoped to buy the
local barber shop
when the owner died
but his son inherited it.

He was the
hair apparent.

I don't know a thing
about working
in an aviary.

I'm going to
wing it.

There was never a doubt I'd get a job selling foreign cars.

It was a *fiat accompli.*

I turned down a job
as a painter after
I learned about
the owner's
brush with the law.

I couldn't join the artists'
island community
until they built
a drawbridge.

I was offered a job
in the military
but I said
no tanks.

I'd only work at a
time-share company
as a last resort.

I'd work at a restaurant without reservations.

I was delighted to be invited back as a meditation instructor.

There's no place like Om.

I said I wasn't happy
that men and women
were not paid equally
at the humor magazine.

The editor promised me
they were working
to achieve parody.

I was unjustly fired
from a restaurant.

That incident really
ate me up.

I got caught stealing
a pillow while working
in furniture repair.

They sent me to
refoam school.

I gave in too quickly while negotiating to sell office supplies.

I didn't want to push the envelope.

I applied at the zoo
for a job feeding the
leopards but they
didn't have a
spot for me.

I did okay selling remedies
for insect bites and
poison ivy once
I realized my
customers were
an itch market.

I screwed up three job
interviews in the same day,
for a dental lab technician,
a stand-up comic,
and a typographer.

I was horrible with
first impressions.

I worked at a
potters' kiln
until I was
fired.

I'm told I was rejected for the job as a tailor for the same reason every other applicant was rejected.

My rejection followed a familiar pattern.

I didn't get the job as
a dress designer
because they said
I wasn't cut from
the right cloth.

I'd love to be a writer but thinking about it brings up too many penned-up emotions.

When I got out of jail
with no job and no
prospects, I didn't
know what
to do next.

I was unaware of my
con sequences.

There are a lot of fears being spread about the airline profession but they're all groundless.

I screwed up on my first day
as a carpenter but on
day two I nailed it.

Unfortunately my boss
was a tool.

I never saw it coming.

I turned down an offer to work in the defense industry.

The owner went ballistic.

It was no one's fault but my own for getting fired from the aquarium after I came in tanked.

Ah, the life of a gillnetter. Smell of fresh air, cool breeze, good exercise. But where could I park my boat at night when I had two alternatives?

It was a real pair o' docks.

I turned down a job offer
to install curtains
because the owners
were so disorganized.

It was like the blinds
leading the blinds.

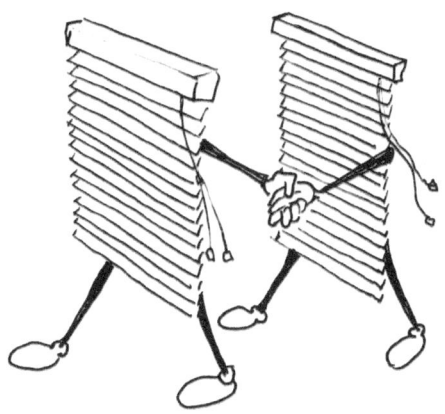

I turned down an offer to be a dentist's receptionist.

It didn't have teeth.

I loved taking care of the elephants when I worked at the zoo. Then my boss made a mistake, blamed me, and I got fired.

Shame on him.
Tusk-tusk.

I was offered a job
selling cottage cheese.

I said no whey.

I was offered a job as
a pheasant hunter.

I said I was game.

The boss at the tobacco company made a lot of promises but he was blowing smoke.

I guess working there was all just a pipe dream.

It was too bad.

I had high expectorations.

I'd like to be a music teacher, but that would be just asking for treble.

Unless they scaled back my workload without reducing my bass salary.

In my short time working
at the physics lab,
I made a mass
of everything.

I didn't do any better gathering honey at the bee hive after I came in buzzed.

My experience as a
lawyer was brief.

Every time I got my salary,
they would docket.

I interviewed to be a
photographer but we
couldn't bring our
negotiations to
a resolution.

I shutter to think how they might have developed.

Then again, maybe I was just too negative.

I've waited long enough
to be a plumber.

It's time to take
the plunge.

To be a civil engineer,
I'd have to be
a dam fool.

Being a professional gambler would bring me to the pinochle of success.

But I don't think it's in the cards for me.

I worked briefly at the comedy club until I got canned.

I'm on track to have a
successful career
on the railroad,
with a salary that
includes all the
bells and whistles.

To spare my feelings,
I didn't pin my hopes on it,
but being a professional
bowler was right
up my alley.

I worked as a gardener
until my boss got
the dirt on me.

He raked me over the coals
and said he was trying
to weed out the
malcontents.

I had no recourse;
he was the
big seed.

I really enjoyed my time
as a chicken farmer.

Unfortunately
I made a poultry living.

I turned down the offer
to be a violinist
in the orchestra.

There were too many
strings attached.

I was invited to join a team of trapeze artists but I couldn't swing it.

When I told my folks I wanted to be a gymnast they flipped and starting hanging out at the bars.

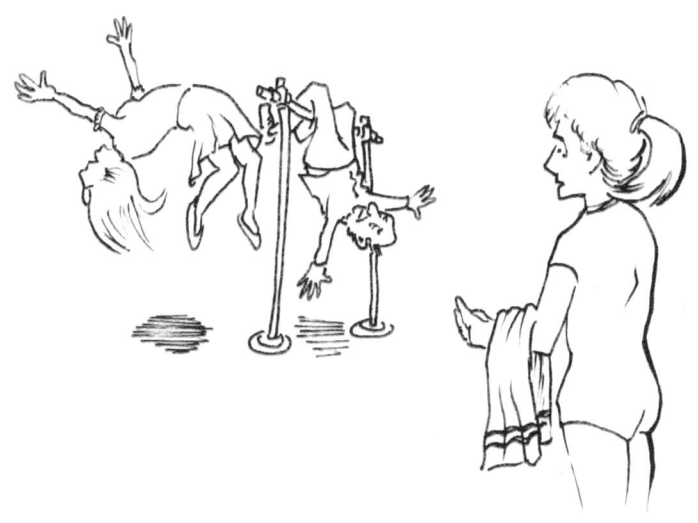

I litterally would love to be a cat sitter.

I littorally would love
to be a lifeguard
or a beach bum.

I got hired at the bakery
because they got a rise
out of my rye
sense of humor.

Unfortunately, I was toast by the time I punched out.

Who kneads a crumby job like that?

I made a noble effort to be a knight watchman but it was feudal.

Fortunately, I was able to serf the web and find another job.

I would have worked as a proctologist's assistant if they had sent me checks in advance.

They were only willing to pay in a-rears.

In hindsight, I should have taken the job.

I was all atwitter
when I got hired
to be a
social network
marketer.

To even think I would milk cows is beyond the pail.

I was totally confident
during my interview
to be a manicurist
and sure enough
I nailed it.

I never heard back on my application to the fishery.

They kept me on the hook.

It was reel annoying.

When my boss fired me
from the Middle Eastern
restaurant, he
made me falafel.

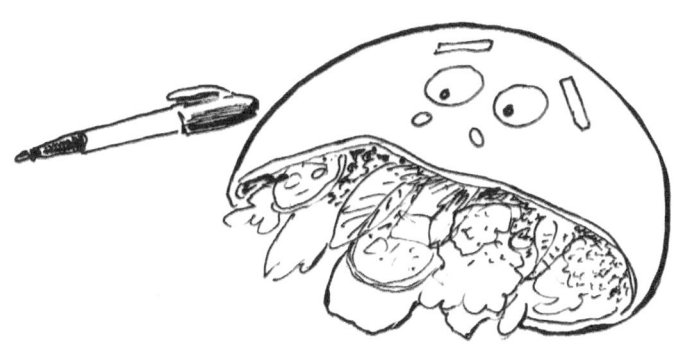

I didn't trust my interviewer at the breakfast diner.

When I presented my terms, he waffled.

I agreed to join the
wrestling team
because I knew
my coach would go
to the mat for me.

Getting me to work in a prison would be a hard cell.

I looked for a job
in real estate.

There were lots available.

FINAL WORD TO READERS

Thank you for purchasing and reading *Ken Wachsberger's Puns and Word Plays for the Job Seeker*. If you found this book enjoyable, please be kind enough to review it on your blog, through your social media networks, or at your favorite retailer so that other readers can find it. Then again, if you didn't enjoy it, go ahead and review it as well. (I just hope there are fewer of you.) It is available as a print-on-demand from Kindle and an ebook from smashwords.com and amazon.com.

ABOUT THE AUTHOR

Ken Wachsberger is a long-time author, editor, story teller, political organizer, and book coach who has written, edited, and lectured on an eclectic range of topics including the Holocaust and Jewish resistance during World War II, the First Amendment, the Vietnam era, writing in the electronic age, copyright, teachers' rights, writers' rights, the I-Search paper, writing for healing and self-discovery. And now puns?

OTHER BOOKS BY KEN WACHSBERGER

For other books by Ken Wachsberger,
please check his websites:

www.azenphonypress.com
www.voicesfromtheunderground.com

www.ingramcontent.com/pod-product-compliance
Lightning Source LLC
Chambersburg PA
CBHW020656300426
44112CB00007B/397